Cuneiform

ANCIENT SCRIPTS

Cuneiform

Irving Finkel and
Jonathan Taylor

J. Paul Getty Museum
Los Angeles

© 2015 The Trustees of the British Museum
Fifth printing

Irving Finkel and Jonathan Taylor have asserted the right to be identified as the authors of this work.

Published in the United States of America by the J. Paul Getty Museum, Los Angeles
Getty Publications
1200 Getty Center Drive, Suite 500
Los Angeles, California 90049-1682
getty.edu/publications

Bobby Birchall, Bobby and Co., *Designer*
Kurt Hauser, *Cover Designer*

Distributed in the United States and Canada by the University of Chicago Press

Printed and bound in China by 1010 Printing Co. Ltd

ISBN 978-1-60606-447-4
Library of Congress Control Number: 2014952411

Published simultaneously in the United Kingdom by
The British Museum Press
A division of The British Museum Company Ltd
The British Museum
Great Russell Street, London WC1B 3DG
britishmuseum.org/publishing

The majority of objects illustrated in this book are from the collection of the British Museum.
The British Museum registration numbers for these objects can be found in the corresponding captions.

Frontispiece: Detail from a palace wall relief dating to the reign of Ashurnasirpal II.
The cuneiform signs to write the king's proclamation march proudly across the very face of the sculpture.
Gypsum, 865-860 BC. H. 232.41 cm; W. 224.79 cm. British Museum 124567.

Contents

Before we start

If you're new to the wonders of cuneiform, here are some key facts to help you start your journey.

What is it?

Cuneiform is a kind of writing, not a language. The word cuneiform comes from Latin *cuneus* 'wedge', and simply means 'wedge shaped'. The word refers to the shape made each time a scribe put stylus to clay. The cuneiform writing system is also not an alphabet, and it doesn't have 'letters'. Instead it used between 600 and 1000 characters to write words (or parts of them) or syllables (or parts of them). It's like writing '&' instead of 'a n d' or 'ca-at' instead of 'c a t'. The two main languages written in cuneiform are Sumerian and Akkadian (from ancient Iraq), although over a dozen others are recorded, most important among them Hittite. Sumerian has no known relations, while Akkadian is related to Arabic and Hebrew. Akkadian comes in two main flavours: Assyrian and Babylonian, which are closely related dialects.

Hittite, written in simplified cuneiform, is related to
European and Indian languages.

When was it around?

Cuneiform traces its roots back to a momentous episode
for the world around 3200 BC when, for the first time ever,
someone came up with the idea of writing. Prehistory
stopped; history began. It continued to be used through
the third, second and first millennia BC, and even into the
first century AD. The distance in time that separates the
latest surviving tablet from us is half that which separates
it from the first cuneiform. Cuneiform specialists (or
'Assyriologists') typically divide all that time into the
following main periods (which are all BC):

Archaic	*c.*3200–*c.*2900
Early Dynastic	*c.*2900–*c.*2300
Old Akkadian	*c.*2300–*c.*2100
Ur III	*c.*2100–*c.*2000
Old Babylonian/Old Assyrian	*c.*2000–*c.*1600
Middle Babylonian/Middle Assyrian	*c.*1600–*c.*900
Neo-Babylonian/Neo-Assyrian	*c.*900–*c.*600
Late Babylonian	539 onwards

These divisions refer to the time periods, the scripts and the
language dialects with roughly equal meaning. The exact
dating of events is still hotly debated for many periods.

Where was it used and by whom?

Cuneiform was used primarily in Mesopotamia ('Between-
the-Rivers') (see p. 9). The name is our catch-all term
for the whole area that is now Iraq and eastern Syria.
During the second and first millennia BC, the south of
Mesopotamia (from around modern Baghdad, down to

the Persian Gulf coast) was known as
Babylonia, while the north was called
Assyria. Earlier, during the third millennium
BC, the area that was later Babylonia was
divided into Akkad in the upper half and
Sumer in the lower half.

Mesopotamian cuneiform was borrowed
by neighbouring cultures. At various points
during the long course of its history, this
writing system came to be used in the west
of modern Iran, Armenia, Turkey, Syria,
Lebanon, Israel, the Palestinian territories,
Egypt, and Bahrain. In two cases (Old
Persian and Ugaritic), it inspired new types
of writing which shared the wedge-shaped
appearance of cuneiform, but worked
completely differently from it.

In this book it is necessary to generalize.
Many cultures lived in Mesopotamia, yet
here we can talk only of 'Sumerians',
'Assyrians', 'Babylonians', or even just
'Mesopotamians'. It is like talking of
'Europeans', 'Americans' or 'Arabs'.
The reader should bear in mind that
reality would be more nuanced.

Fig. 1 Map of the
Middle East.

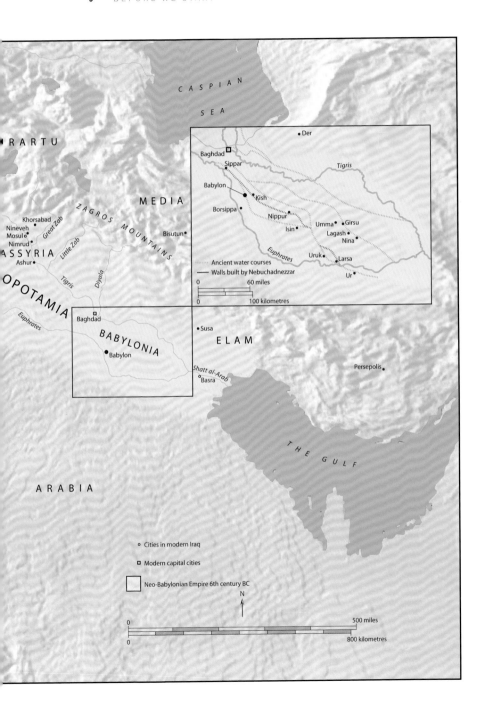

C A S P I A N
S E A

RARTU

MEDIA

ZAGROS MOUNTAINS

Khorsabad
Nineveh
Mosul
Nimrud
Ashur
Great Zab
Little Zab
Bisutun

ASSYRIA

Tigris
Diyala

OPOTAMIA

Euphrates

Baghdad

BABYLONIA
Babylon

Susa

ELAM

Shatt al-Arab
Basra

Persepolis

T H E   G U L F

ARABIA

Der
Baghdad
Sippar
Tigris
Babylon
Kish
Borsippa
Nippur
Isin
Umma
Girsu
Lagash
Nina
Euphrates
Uruk
Larsa
Ur

.... Ancient water courses
——— Walls built by Nebuchadnezzar

0   60 miles
0   100 kilometres

○ Cities in modern Iraq

□ Modern capital cities

▢ Neo-Babylonian Empire 6th century BC

N
↑

0   500 miles
0   800 kilometres

CHAPTER ONE

Looking backwards and forwards

The Mesopotamians revelled in the great antiquity of their civilizations. Schoolchildren learnt the stories of great kings of the past. Scribes delighted in finding old tablets. Was it a message from the distant past or a long lost piece of wisdom? Some texts were valued as the work of scholars from bygone days, others seen to be written by the gods themselves. One text was even said to have been dictated by a horse.

Origins

A story from about 1800 BC told how long ago Enmerkar, king of the ancient city of Uruk, was locked in a battle of wits with a rival who lived across the mountains. He invented cuneiform writing specially to help his messenger remember ever more complicated messages. His enemy, the Lord of Aratta, a mythical city far to the east, stared at the tablet, scratched his head in puzzlement, and was forced to submit. Another story from that time tells how Sargon (later to become the

Fig. 2 The earliest known texts are not letters but administrative documents. They often record rations (see encircled sign of head and bowl) issued to workers. The signs are arranged in boxes; the helpful practice of writing in lines, with the characters in reading order, did not appear until almost a thousand years later (see fig. 3). Clay, c.3100 BC. 7.5 x 4.5 cm. British Museum 140852.

famous king of Akkad) was sent by his sovereign as messenger to another king of Uruk, Lugalzagesi. He carried his own death sentence, concealed within the world's first envelope.

Today we know that cuneiform was already centuries old by the time of Enmerkar and Sargon. It seems to have been invented in around 3200 BC at Uruk, as a bookkeeping tool. Temple accountants used a system of written signs, many of which were more or less realistic drawings, to keep track of rations of beer and bread, and to monitor flocks of sheep and goats. They would have had no idea of the incredible power of the tool they had just invented. It was several centuries later until the first

inscriptions of kings, letters and literature. But cuneiform soon spread across the Middle East and was continuously used for over 3,000 years.

The very earliest texts were written with a narrow stylus. At this stage, we can call the signs pictographic. In many cases they are easy to identify, and everything is depicted the right way up. Two interesting things happened as the early script evolved. The design of each sign became more linear and stylized as scribes preferred a different-shaped and thicker stylus where the wedge itself became more pronounced. By the time of the mature script, all signs were made of true wedges. Secondly, there was a wholesale change in the orientation of the writing itself. This seems to have come in at some point in the late third or early second millennium BC, and all scribes began to write as if their cuneiform signs had each turned 90 degrees anticlockwise. No one quite knows when or why this happened.

Time capsules

Most tablets needed to be useful for only a short time: maybe a few hours or days at school, or a few years for a letter, loan or account. Legal texts were needed for rather longer. People who bought property received house deeds proving the chain of possession back up to a century or two. Despite having been discarded, such relatively ephemeral documents survive by accident in huge numbers. From our point of view, each is a time capsule.

The Mesopotamians gave much thought to the past and the future, and some of their inscriptions were designed to last for a very long time. This is evident from special inscriptions buried within the structure of temples, palaces or city walls. Rulers made sure that their name and achievements were recorded whenever they engaged in a building project. The intention was that future generations

Fig. 3 A list of payments of silver to five people, dating from the reign of Lugalzagesi of Uruk (c.2300 BC). By now the cuneiform had taken on its characteristic wedge-shaped appearance. Clay, c.2340 BC. 4.8 x 5.7 cm. British Museum 114362.

would find these records during their own construction work. In some cases almost 2,000 years were bridged in this way. The later scribes would study the old text before re-burying it, together with a contemporary equivalent. The texts promised rewards for a later ruler who would honour his forebear. These messages for the future achieved their purpose better than their authors could ever have dreamed. Now they help modern scholars understand who was who, and what they achieved.

Inscribed clay nails formed part of a cluster of objects deposited together in the walls of temples during the third millennium (see fig. 4). This unusual shape derives from the use of clay nails to indicate ownership of a building. The

Fig. 4 Inscribed nail referring to a political alliance between two rulers (see p. 15). Clay, c.2400 BC. L. 26.7 cm. British Museum 121208.

size and shape of such objects differed between cities and over time, and rulers must have chosen the characteristics they preferred. The example shown in fig. 4 carries an inscription of Enmetena, ruler of Lagash in around 2400 BC. It records his alliance with Lugalkiginedudu of Uruk, one of the earliest documented examples of a formal relationship between states.

Mud bricks were an opportunity too good to miss. From around 2300 BC, scribes were put to work writing out royal names and titles on uncountable building blocks. Then somebody had a bright idea: a true labour-saving device. Signs that made up the king's inscription could be cut in reverse on a block and used to stamp the bricks (fig. 5). This first kind of printing went on for almost two thousand years. Remarkably, its use was reserved for mundane bricks, and no other purpose. Other types of text were not required in large numbers and there may also have been cultural resistance to the use of stamping for learned texts. In a few stamped examples some signs are upside down. The best explanation is perhaps that individually mounted wedge signs had been carelessly replaced in the matrix after cleaning out the stamp. Here we would have not only printing, but even moveable type, two thousand years before Gutenberg!

Fig. 6 is a stamped inscription of King Nebuchadnezzar II of Babylon (604–562 BC), listing his royal titles and proudly declaring his parentage. Huge numbers of these bricks were needed for the many large scale construction projects undertaken by Nebuchadnezzar in his capital city. Some were marked in alphabetic Aramaic letters specifying the factory where they were made, presumably for quality control purposes. Such bricks were the building blocks of the temple tower that was the reality behind the Biblical Tower of Babel. Being both readily accessible and unusually interesting, they were among the first inscriptions collected by Europeans during the rediscovery of Mesopotamia. This one belonged to the British diplomat (in Baghdad) and antiquarian scholar Claudius Rich, and was collected around 1811.

Ye olde cuneiforme

Babylonians treasured the longevity of their civilization. When King Nebuchadnezzar II asserted that everything he says in his inscription is true, he was borrowing an expression last used 1600 years earlier. King Nabonidus, the last native king of Babylon (555–539 BC), is famous for his interest in the past, recreating long obsolete roles and practices. He sought out old inscriptions with particular relish, apparently in the course of major religious reform.

Fig. 6 Brick (with detail) bearing the inscription of King Nebuchadnezzar II of Babylon (604–562 BC). Clay, c.600 BC. 32 x 32.5 cm. British Museum 90081.

Figs 7 and 8 These two tablets are both copies made by Bel-ushallim, son of Abibi, the exorcist: one is a copy of an inscription of King Ammiditana (c.1683–1647 BC), the other an old magic spell against gall. One was part of receiving a solid education; the other of direct practical use. Clay, c.6th century BC. 6.2 x 6.9 cm and 7 x 11.3 cm. British Museum 38303 and 47859.

Apprentice scribes sometimes had to copy and study old inscriptions. We have dozens of tablets produced by young scribes who visited temples or ruins in search of them. They copied the ancient texts as carefully as possible, making efforts to reproduce the archaic handwriting. One scribe even records that individual cuneiform signs he was copying were incompletely preserved. The next step was to read the text and translate any Sumerian into modern Akkadian. Often the scribe would make a note to record where he found the text – 'According to an old stone monument which was in the city of Sippar', for example (see figs 7 and 8).

Reading old inscriptions was never entirely straightforward; just think how much help modern readers of English need to understand Shakespeare, Chaucer or Bede. Many of the cuneiform inscriptions were written in Sumerian, a language unrelated to Akkadian, and by then restricted to scholarly circles. Akkadian itself had naturally changed over time, not just in the creation of new words, loss of old ones and change of meaning of others, but also in the way the words were put together in sentences. This is one of the reasons behind the continued copying of old lists of words (see chapter 4) and the creation of learned commentaries to interpret them. And by the seventh century BC, Aramaic was beginning to replace Akkadian as the mother tongue of Mesopotamians. But before the scribe could even start to grapple with these difficulties, he had first to be able to read the handwriting, which itself had changed a lot over the centuries. The ability to read old inscriptions was a hard-earned and cherished skill. The study of handwriting was highly developed; scholarly lists set old signs against their current versions. An example of such a list is shown in fig. 9.

This compendium of signs represents the fruit of intense scholarship. It matches up archaic signs with their contemporary counterparts. Some are accurate renderings of sign forms we have found on old tablets. Others have been dismissed as fantasy, although new tablets now suggest that they may be real after all. It also lists the secret number for each sign, used for encoding omens and other texts.

Expertise in handwriting was useful when it came to making new texts. As today, it was normal to write commemorative texts in an old-fashioned looking style. This was more than just making them look quaint; it enhanced the authority and prestige of the rulers,

Fig. 9 List setting old cuneiform signs against their current versions. Clay, c.450 BC. 4.7 x 9.4 cm. British Museum 46603.

associating them with the deep past. Scribes could also use their knowledge to create fake texts that pretended to be much older than they actually were. The most famous example of this is the 'Cruciform Monument of Manishtushu', which pretends to be an inscription of Manishtushu, a twenty-third century BC ruler (fig. 10). While the strange shape and old-looking writing lend the monument the appearance of antiquity, the reality was very different, as is revealed by study of the language used. It was manufactured sometime in the first millennium BC to provide a solid precedent in support of privileges and offerings for the temple in the city of Sippar.

Fig. 10 The 'Cruciform Monument of Manishtushu'. Stone, c.6th century BC. 11 x 21 cm. British Museum 91022.

CHAPTER TWO

Going to school

The best days of their lives?

Learning how to read and write cuneiform was a long and often painful process. Under the watchful eye of their father or uncle, the young children (usually boys) of a scribe would copy, memorize and recite a long series of schoolbooks. Several years and a good many beatings later, they would emerge as walking encyclopaedias of knowledge, dextrously manipulating cuneiform to reveal and transmit meaning. But first, there was much to learn.

Our clearest picture of 'school' life comes from the Babylonian city of Nippur. Archaeologists excavated a private house there containing hundreds of exercise books that had been thrown away in the eighteenth century BC. We can see how students advanced from practising their ABCs through writing names and words and onto studying difficult literature. The first exercises drilled the child in how to handle the stylus, making single wedges – first the vertical, then the horizontal, then the corner wedge, again and again and again. Then they needed to know how to combine the individual strokes to make whole characters,

Fig. 11 Spelling practice with personal names. Above, the teacher's neat example; below, the pupil's faltering attempt to copy it. Clay, from Ur, c.1800 BC. Diam. 9.4 cm. British Museum UET 6.792.

starting with very simple ones containing just two or three strokes, before moving on to more difficult combinations needing eight or more strokes of the stylus. Then the students chanted *too-tah-tee*, *boo-bah-bee*, *noo-nah-nee*, learning how the signs captured the sounds of speech. The first real meaning came through writing people's names. From there it was a short step to putting signs together to make words: long lists of plants, animals, stones and stars. These were memorized, section by section until the pupil had learnt everything by heart.

While learning vocabulary and practising spelling, good handwriting was also essential. On the tablet shown in fig. 11, the teacher wrote three names. The pupil memorized them, and on the other side tried to reproduce them. He wrote them in reverse order, and his handwriting lacks the fluency and control displayed by his teacher. Tablets like this fit into the palm of a hand, and were made by squashing a ball of clay between the hands or against a flat surface.

Along the way the student learnt the subtleties of cuneiform. Signs could be used in different ways, and each could have several readings (see chapter 7 for more detail). Signs could be combined, giving spellings which were not always predictable in reading; there was a special list explaining these. Words were then strung into sentences and practised through proverbs, such as 'A loving heart builds houses'. These short sayings gave a good introduction to what lay ahead. Being young children, an opportunity to misread a text as a fart joke was too hard to pass up; how much funnier they would have found it had they realized that four thousand years later it would be discussed by learned professors and lovingly preserved in a museum collection for future generations. Having mastered the basics of reading and writing, the young apprentice studied literature. Hymns in praise of kings indoctrinated the next generation of officials. Future priests practised the liturgies. And all of this with a focus on the Sumerian language, used for scholarly and religious purposes, but no longer commonly heard on the streets.

Alongside 'citizenship training' through hymns, myths and law codes, schoolboys learnt how to debate. They trained on texts arguing the benefits to mankind of antagonistic pairs: winter and summer, sheep and grain or bird and fish. They also read texts about the exploits of trainee scribes, and their sometimes difficult relations with each other and their teachers. We don't know much about polite conversation in Sumerian (how did you say 'please' or 'thank you'?), but we can swear and insult each

Fig. 12 Having written out the tale about a *Lazy Slave Girl*, a fed-up young student couldn't resist the urge to immortalize his teacher on the back of his tablet. Is that a cane he is brandishing? Clay, *c.*1800 BC. 7.4 x 8.9 cm. Frau Professor Hilprecht Collection of Babylonian Antiquities in the possession of the University of Jena, Germany. HS 1448.

other with great vigour. Were we to travel back in time and meet a Sumerian, our first encounter would not go well.

The Sumerian *Schooldays* (fig. 13) offers a literary picture of life at school, one that did not necessarily reflect the reality of the time accurately:

> – *Schoolboy, where did you go from earliest days?*
> – *I went to school.*
> – *What did you do at school?*
> – *I read my tablet, ate my lunch, prepared my tablet, wrote it, finished it; then my set lines were prepared for me, [and in] the afternoon my hand copies were prepared for me. When school broke up for the day, I went home, entered the house; [there] was my father sitting. I told my father about my hand copies, then read the tablet to him. My father was pleased; truly I found favour with my father.*

The next day the boy suffers a terrible day. Everything goes wrong and he is beaten repeatedly. His father invites the teacher for dinner, plies him with drink and gives him presents. The teacher responds by praising the boy's dedication, and wishing him well in all his tasks.

One for the gods

Fast forward a thousand years or so and young boys in the city of Babylon were still battling with lists. Some of the old lists of signs and words were still in circulation, but now they had taken on a very different use – as scholarly tools to help understand the traditional learned texts. The new schoolbooks show a curriculum of short exercises not so different in nature from what their predecessors had endured (fig. 14). Young boys practised wedge after wedge, sign after sign, name after name, word after word. Then they graduated from these simple exercises on large tablets (up to 25 cm long) to smaller

Fig. 13 *Schooldays.* This Sumerian tale paints a picture of school life. Clay, from Nippur, Iraq. Penn Museum, University of Pennsylvania. CBS 6094.

tablets where they practised literature, prayers, magic and medicine. The final element of training seems to have been a work placement with an uncle, copying out reference books and learning the family profession – exorcist, diviner, cult singer or astronomer.

Some school tablets contain notes stating that they had been dedicated to Nabu, Babylonian god of writing, and kept in his temple. They ask for good health and wealth, and the wellbeing of the family. These dedications were maybe part of a ceremony marking certain milestones in a boy's school career. They could be carefully decorated with borders made of wedge impressions.

Fig. 14 A typical exercise tablet dating from the time when the Greeks ruled in Babylon. The back of the tablet contains practice administrative texts, one of which helpfully names King Philip Arrhidaeus (c.323–317 BC). Clay. 15.1 x 13.2 cm. British Museum 33838.

CHAPTER THREE

Who used cuneiform writing?

Functional literacy

In the modern world literacy is taken for granted, but this was never the case in Mesopotamia. Professional scribes generally did most of the writing. Insight into everyday experience comes from letters, both official and private. Person A dictated his letter to a scribe, who wrote it out on a tablet. The tablet was delivered to B, who had it read out for him. This is evident from the word for letter, *unedukku* in Akkadian, borrowed from Sumerian, *u-na-dug*, which means 'say-to-him!' and letters accordingly often begin: *To Mr A speak! Thus says Mr B...*

Use of this formula does not necessarily mean, of course, that Mr A and Mr B were incapable of writing or reading for themselves, especially if the correspondents were of a higher social class functioning in a sophisticated urban background. Most trained scribes whom we know of were men. King Sargon of Agade's famous daughter Enheduanna (*c.*2285–2250 BC) was a scribe and an author too, and we know the names of a few female scribes in subsequent periods, but not many.

Fig. 15 Another famous banking family were the Murashus of fifth-century BC Nippur. This is one of their dealing records (in cuneiform Akkadian) with a note beneath in alphabetic Aramaic to allow swift retrieval when needed. Clay, 5th century BC, from Nippur, Iraq. Penn Museum, University of Pennsylvania. CBS 6132.

Traditionally it has been assumed that at any given point in Mesopotamian history, only a minority of the population was literate, and broadly speaking this must be true. But it is necessary to guard against exaggeration. Recent research shows that literacy in various forms was more widespread. While full mastery of the script can only have been acquired through that long course of teaching, lower levels of literacy were still functional for everyday purposes. We can be sure that powerful families such as the Egibi bankers of Babylon from the beginning of the seventh century BC always had a son or nephew who was capable of keeping the books, administering rent records and arranging the import of costly drugs from Arabia; perhaps literacy was transmitted privately within such a family.

Unlike modern students of cuneiform, who
must learn not just the signs but also the
ancient languages as well, people who
lived in the ancient cuneiform world
faced a much less daunting prospect.
The claim of the Assyrian king
Ashurbanipal (668–c.627 BC) that he
could read inscriptions from before the
Flood, 'unlike the kings who went before
me,' has lent credence to the idea that even the

Assyrian kings couldn't read as a rule. While we know from beginner's exercises kept in his library that he himself was an exceptionally interested and able student, it is gratuitous to suppose, on the basis of such a remark, that his father and grandfather before him were unable to read the inscriptions on their own palace sculptures.

In fact the writing of a letter or a legal statement required working knowledge of fewer than two hundred cuneiform signs, so realistically many people could have recognized common signs. The range of reading abilities would vary tremendously from place to place and period to period. Letters and documents from the close-knit community of Assyrian merchant families (figs 16–18) operating between Assyria and Anatolia in the nineteenth century BC show that non-professional scribes could

Figs 16–18 (Left) A merchant letter, with a postscript on a small piece of extra clay, and the envelope in which they would have fitted inside (right) bearing seal impressions. Scribes usually fitted everything on their tablet. Here, exceptionally, a non-professional scribe was slightly miscalculated. (In reality, the script in fig. 17 would have been the same size as that shown in fig. 16 above.) Letter: clay, c.19th century BC. 5.7 x 6.7 cm. British Museum 113573.

communicate in writing very effectively. Many letters there are to or from women, showing the ready availability of writing to the whole community.

Libraries and archives

Tablets are only infrequently found *in situ*, that is, just as they were left by their previous owners. We know that archives were often kept in baskets, boxes or vessels, and family archives from the second and first millennia can survive in great abundance. Institutions such as temples certainly had their own libraries; the most illuminating find of this kind was an intact library at the city of Sippar, which revealed a large collection of tablets stored on end in neat alcoves in the walls (fig. 20). Great finds of tablets have sometimes been made of the written work of several generations of one scribal family. Two remarkable cases are those of the much later Shangu-Ninurta and Ekur-zakir families at the city of Uruk, from whose archives abundant literary and scholarly tablets have been recovered, in outstandingly high-quality copies. One particularly welcome type of inscription is the tablet catalogue, in

Fig. 20 The library
found in the 1980s
during Iraqi excavations
at Sippar's temple of
the sungod. On
discovery, tablets were
still neatly arranged on
their shelves, as they
had been left when the
last librarian finished
work 2,500 years ago.

which the compositions in a particular library are listed, as if with us in mind. Survivals include catalogues of Sumerian literary tablets from the Old Babylonian period (see p. 7), and more from the first millennium, such as an extraordinary breakdown of medical compositions that were available in one library at the city of Ashur. This gives not only the different titles of the medical works, but also the number of tablets from which they were constituted, and the first line of each. Another such catalogue details the first line of each of the thirty-two tablets of the dictionary known as *Nabnitu*, 'Form.' What can be an awful headache is when the tablet numbers in such a catalogue are not borne out by the known tablets themselves; this can reflect internal editing, or the separate traditions of different cities, but it can be hard on us, two and a half thousand years later, trying to make order out of chaos with a pile of inconsistent tablets, half of which are broken at the crucial point.

Fig. 21 This rounded tablet is inscribed with the first lines of many classical liturgies (called *ershemmas*) in Sumerian. Clay, c.18th century BC. 8.7 x 6.9 cm. British Museum 23771.

CHAPTER FOUR

How do we understand it, anyway?

When people encounter cuneiform writing on a clay tablet or a stone sculpture for the first time they are usually sceptical that such stuff can be 'real' writing at all. If an earnest curator manages to persuade them, there are natural follow-up questions: how was it deciphered in the first place and how do we know what the signs mean or what they sound like?

Eureka! The decipherment

Cuneiform was extinct for almost two thousand years; it had to be deciphered from scratch and the achievement was nothing short of heroic. When the first translations appeared in print certain university professors of Arabic or Classics were inclined to disparage barbaric-looking cuneiform and those who claimed to understand it, unwilling to come to terms with this upstart discipline. In 1857 the Royal Asiatic Society in London hosted a competition to settle the matter: four leading scholars (Henry Creswicke Rawlinson, Edward Hincks, Jules

Oppert and Henry Fox Talbot) each submitted an independent translation of a long military account in Assyrian cuneiform; the level of similarity that resulted sufficed for the distinguished panel to declare that decipherment had truly been achieved. With that the great work of reading tablets could continue uninhibitedly, and it is still going on.

The decipherment of cuneiform, like that of Egyptian hieroglyphs at much the same time, would have remained impossible without a 'crib' to a more familiar language. In both cases transcription of personal names from one script to another provided the first glimpse of how ancient signs worked. With Babylonian, the trilingual cuneiform inscription in Old Persian, Babylonian and Elamite of the Persian king Darius (522–486 BC) on a mountain pass at Bisutun in Eastern Iran offered the same opportunity as did the Rosetta Stone for hieroglyphs. An earlier breakthrough with Old Persian (via modern Persian) meant that the name of Darius, pronounced *Dariawush*, and repetitive expressions such as 'great king' and 'king of kings,' could now be located within the corresponding panel of Babylonian cuneiform. Given the first syllables such as *da-* and *ri-*, coupled with the justified suspicion that Babylonian might be a Semitic language (like Hebrew and Arabic), put the decipherers on the right road.

That road, however, was to be long and full of obstacles. The decipherers had to realize that this system of writing in wedges was used for more than one language, Sumerian and Akkadian, and the sentences that they were struggling with were often written in a mixture of the two. It was a long time before everybody agreed that the mysterious Sumerian that was gradually emerging into view was a real language at all: it was strikingly different from Semitic Babylonian, and the recovery of its grammar and vocabulary has been a very arduous matter.

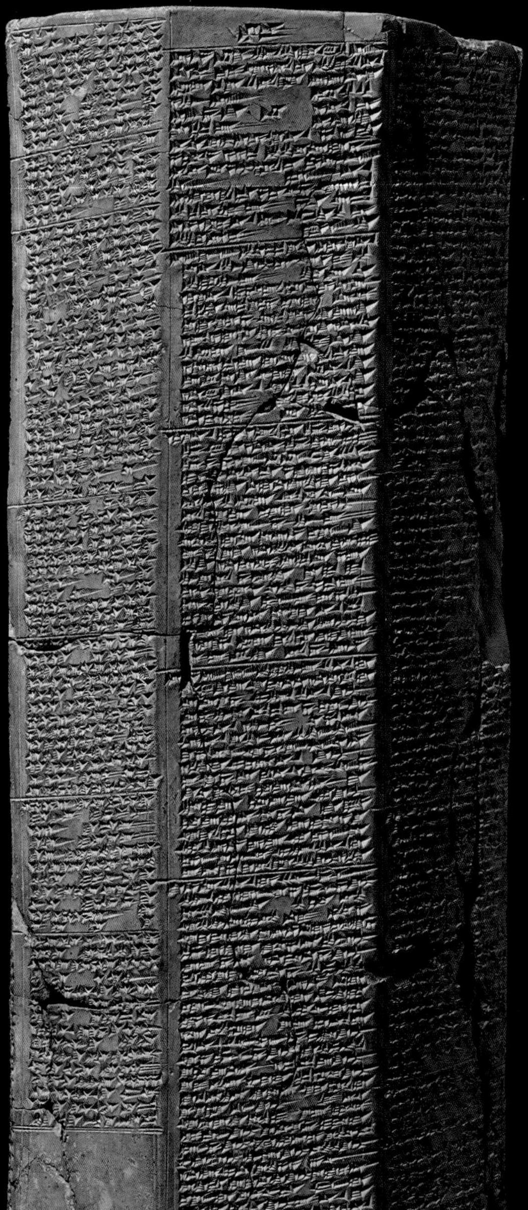

Fig. 22 (left) A magnificent prism of Tiglath-Pileser I (1114–1076 BC), containing an account of his military successes and construction programme. As a long and newly discovered text, it was a good subject for the 1857 competition to demonstrate the fact of cuneiform's decipherment. Clay. 17.8 x 39.4 cm. British Museum K 1621a.

Fig. 23 (above) This giant 'HEAD' sign (highlighted) helped ancient and modern scholars alike to find where to start reading. Detail of fig. 22.

Words in cuneiform tend to be written in a continuous line without breaks, helpful neither for the decipherer nor the beginner student today. Gradually what we now take for granted came to be appreciated; any given cuneiform sign could have more than one sound value and more than one meaning, and a given sound could be expressed by more than one sign. This aspect of the nature of cuneiform signs was unsuspected until the pioneers discovered duplicates of one and the same text in which identical words were spelled differently. One by one, new signs and new readings could be added to the list.

The process of cuneiform decipherment was thus multi-layered, for it demanded full grasp of how signs with multiple possible readings could function as writing, and the reconstruction of two unrelated and very dead languages. The achievement was, therefore, far greater than the decipherment of Egyptian hieroglyphic writing or Mycenaean Linear B.

In the footsteps of the scribes

Amid all this struggle, help came from an unexpected quarter. The scribes who wrote cuneiform tablets for a living and themselves coped daily with its inherent difficulties bequeathed us a range of literally indispensable tools: a whole shelf of cuneiform 'reference books.'

Foremost among these are the lists of signs and words. Lists of words by type or association appear right at the beginning of Mesopotamian writing: as specific signs were developed and agreed on they had to be collected and listed so that they would not be forgotten or confused. Object words for stones, wood or reed were carefully itemized in this way, as were the names of the gods, or the categories of human activities. For the same reasons the individual cuneiform signs were also listed, their distinct sounds written out one by one, so that the full use of a given sign could be readily mastered. Each sign also had its own special name. By way of example, in the following line the scholar explains this with regard to the signs for 'divine weapon':

1.	2.	3.	4.
mi-it-ta	TUKUL.DINGIR	*tu-kul di-gi-ra-ku*	*kak-ku ša ili* (DINGIR)

We learn that the signs TUKUL ('weapon') and DINGIR ('god') put together mean 'divine weapon'. 'Divine weapon' in Sumerian is *mitta* (1.). The special name of the sign TUKUL.DINGIR (2.) is *tukul dingirakku* (3.), meaning '*dingir*-ized *tukul*'. The Akkadian for 'divine weapon' is *kakku* ('weapon') *ša* ('of') *ili* ('god') (4.).

Such lists embodied the very core of cuneiform knowledge, and students had to study them over the following three thousand years. Over that period the lists were naturally extended and developed. What was at first a list of Sumerian words would often be furnished with Akkadian translations, perhaps with the unspoken

Fig. 24 A perfect tablet from a master scribe, giving signs, pronunciations and meanings. This copy was made during the reign of the Persian king Artaxerxes I (465–424 BC), illustrating the continued flourishing of cuneiform culture even after the fall of the last native Babylonian rulers. If all our documents looked like this, Assyriology would almost be easy. Clay. 8.9 x 15.6 cm. British Museum 92693.

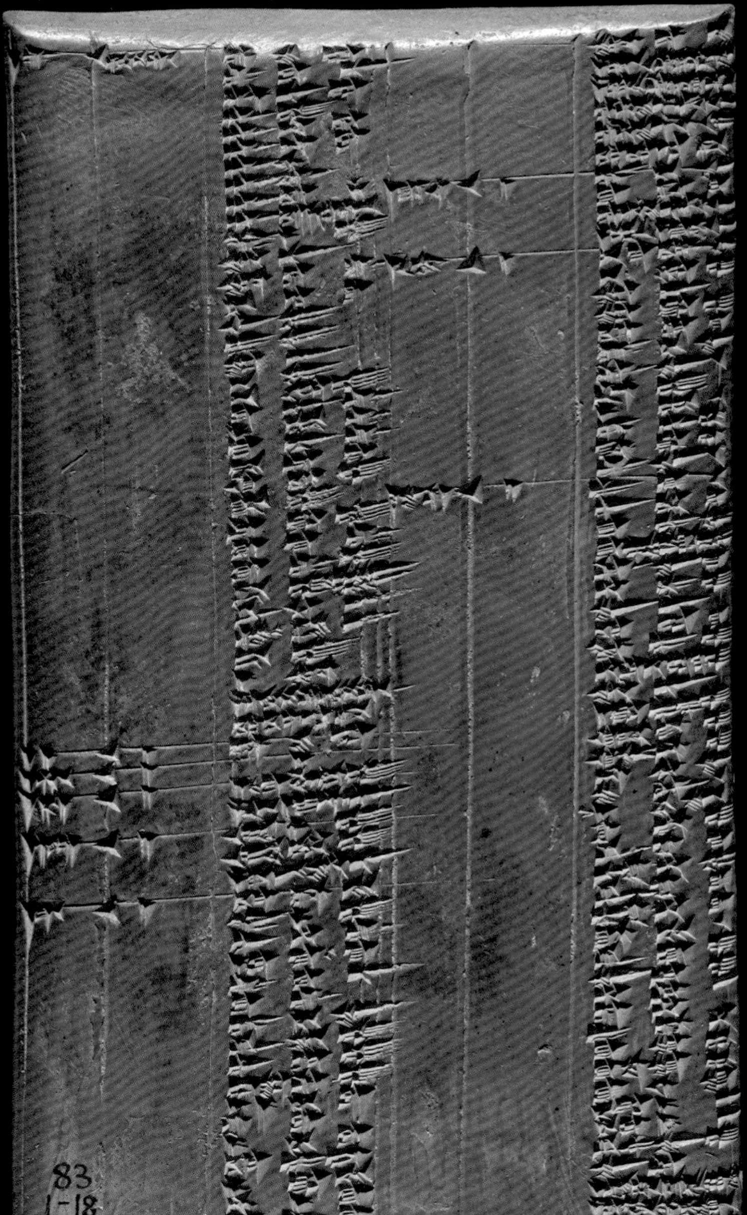
83
1-18
1336.

Fig. 25 This long, thin
tablet is a fine example
of a bilingual literary
text. What was
originally a Sumerian
cult song called
ershemma has been
supplied with a
line-by-line Akkadian
translation, which is
inset to make it
clearer. Neo-Assyrian.
Clay, 7th century BC.
7.9 x 20.2 cm. British
Museum K.2811.

plan behind it all that every word and every sign would be covered in one or other of them. The great compilations were ultimately ordered into tidy series, with numbers of lines and chapter headings, so that retrieval of information was as convenient as possible.

The rather unusual, two-language heritage of ancient Mesopotamia had many consequences. Sumerian and Akkadian lived side by side and students had to study both, for a great proportion of national literature remained encapsulated in Sumerian even as this language began to disappear from daily usage by the early second millennium BC. As a result, Sumerian texts often needed to be translated into Akkadian, first by glossing odd difficult words, but eventually in fully developed bilingual form. The existence of such bilinguals facilitated the classroom teaching of both languages, and also generated sophisticated grammatical analysis by the teachers. Here the individual elements which were combined to write long Sumerian verb forms were identified with their Akkadian equivalents so that modern-looking grammatical paradigms resulted, such as,

Sumerian	Akkadian	
an-gar	*šakin*	It is placed
an-gar-re-en	*šaknāku*	I am placed
an-gar-re-en	*šaknāta*	You are placed
ba-ab-gar	*šuškun*	It is caused to be placed
ba-ab-gar-re-en	*šuškunāku*	I am caused to be placed

Ancient dictionaries, signs lists and bilingual texts (fig. 25) thus provided the modern decipherers with a veritable toolbox, and as mastery of the signs increased (and broken pieces of tablets in museums were put together), it became possible to make use of them directly in reading and understanding inscriptions, just as was done originally in antiquity.

Repositories of knowledge

Identifying duplicate copies is still central to the work of the Assyriologist, for the majority of the tablets available to us today are broken or fragmentary, but among large collections, such as that of the British Museum, there is always the chance of joining one piece to another, or finding a second copy to fill in a tantalising gap. Much of the early cuneiform work in modern times was carried out on tablets from the royal library at Nineveh, once the pride and joy of the great king and scholar Ashurbanipal (668–c.627 BC). The library, some 30,000 tablets and fragments, was excavated under permit by Sir Austen Henry Layard and Hormuzd Rassam, and brought to London to the British Museum, where it became the cornerstone of modern Assyriology. The Nineveh library was something extraordinary in the history of the world. The king had conceived the idea of bringing together and storing the whole of cuneiform knowledge under one roof, anticipating thereby the library of scrolls at Alexandria, and he took a personal interest in everything to do with his tablet collections. Early cuneiform scholars had the great good fortune to inherit a state-of-the-art cuneiform library written in the best possible handwriting. When Nineveh fell to the Medes in 612 BC, Ashurbanipal's tablets were broken and burnt. Ironically, this onslaught ensured their survival; for a library of clay is the only type where a fire is beneficial, baking the tablets hard rather than destroying them. 'Joins' between fragments, the triumph of an Assyriologist's day, are discovered regularly (fig. 26), and work on the precious riches left to us by the great librarian continues to this day.

Fig. 26 So far five pieces of this library tablet have been identified and joined: the great jigsaw puzzle goes on and on. See detail overleaf. Clay, 7th century BC. 10.2 x 21.5 cm. British Museum K.59.

The Nineveh library contained the fullest variety of writings, from high literature to mundane administration. We have myths and epics, hymns and prayers, magical and medical texts, state records, astrological and astronomical texts, and any number of collections of omens, which

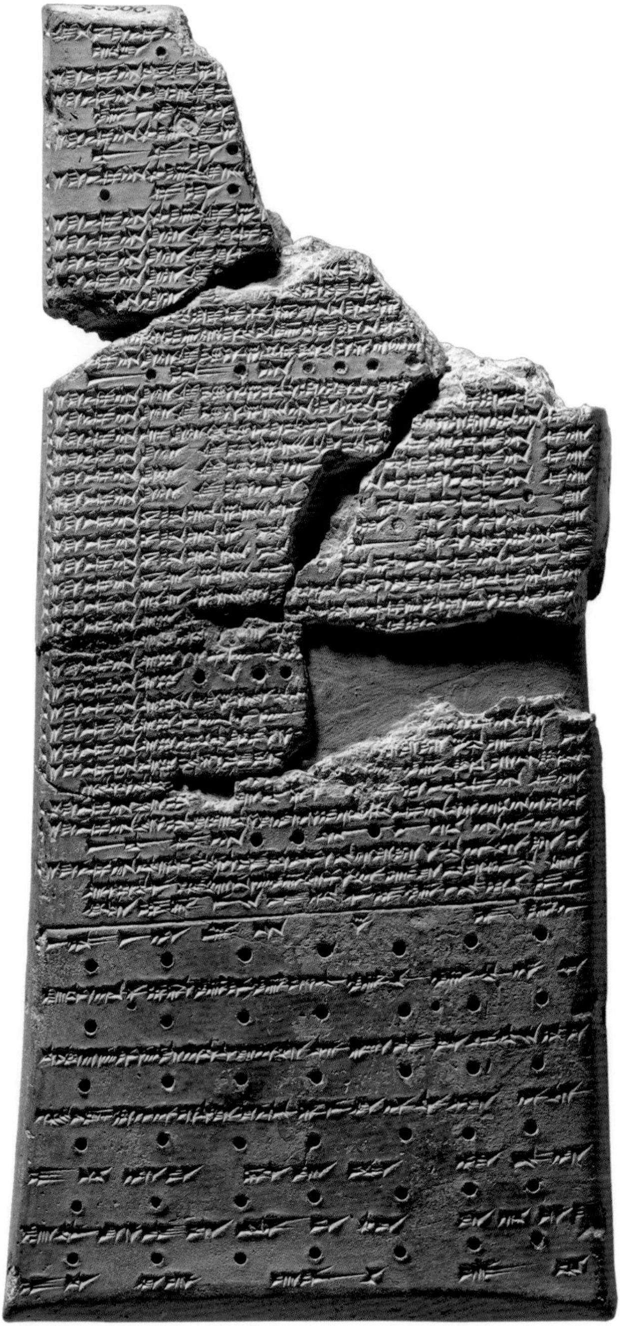

Fig. 27
(Detail from fig. 26)
The double-spaced
lines at the bottom are
the king's ownership
colophon. The empty
spaces have been
'cancelled' with round
holes.

Fig. 28 (Opposite)
The worst casualty
from the hottest part of
the fire: the clay has
vitrified dramatically in
the heat, bubbling and
melting. Clay, 7th
century BC. 17.1 x
16.5 cm. British
Museum K.5967.

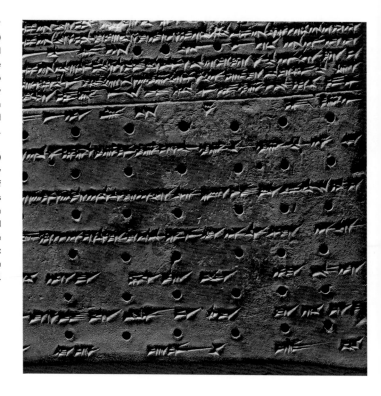

were designed to help the court authorities predict
what was going to happen. Also included are the royal
editions of the indispensable sign lists and word lists.
Modern sign lists and dictionaries are crucially dependent
on Ashurbanipal's ancient lists, and no one can work
without them.

CHAPTER FIVE

The scribe revealed

If we could but meet one of those old Mesopotamian tablet writers, a *ṭupšarru*, in person, how interesting the conversation would be; despite the vast number of surviving tablets, it is hard to get a sense of the individual tablet writer. We would have a hundred questions.

A family affair

Scribal training exemplified discipline steeped in tradition and apprentices must have been discouraged from using writing on clay tablets for experiment and invention because examples of such things are exceptionally rare. As a general rule, scribes (probably) came from scribal families. We know a good deal about their day-to-day school curriculum at certain periods, and we can deduce that graduating scribes will have varied in ability, with the more talented or ambitious going into professions where writing was essential, such as divination or the priesthood, and others earning their keep writing letters and contracts.

Scribes operated with a blend of confidence and concentration, for no one wanted to have to start over with a clean copy. They developed various techniques to help them. For example, with long compositions a small single oblique wedge could be added in the margin every ten lines, and the line total often included at the end, to ensure against omissions. There are other small glimpses of the scribe about his business, in particular the notes in miniature signs that such and such a line had not been seen, or marks to indicate the spots where the tablet that he was copying from was damaged or illegible. To be a cuneiform teacher of distinction implied the mastery of prodigious quantities of texts. Very probably the sign lists and word lists were simply committed to memory by the most able, and any specialism would have its own additional copious resources. The principal concern of the properly trained Mesopotamian intellectual scribe was to preserve and transmit inherited lore, with the inbuilt rider that the older a document the better.

Shhh! It's a secret

Specialist professions such as the arts of healing or predicting the future seem to have had something of the guild structure about them, especially in view of the warnings in the *colophon* – or library docket – that the content is supposed to be safeguarded from the wrong eyes:

> *One who is in the know should only show the tablet to one who is in the know; one who is not in the know must not see it.*

Notwithstanding this stricture, Assyriologists are always very keen to see a tablet colophon, for they are always informative and sometimes extremely revealing. Standard information included is the number of lines, and the name of and number within a composition series (such as *He Who*

Saw Everything, the first line of the famous Gilgamesh story, which comes to us in twelve numbered tablets). Here, too, sometimes the secrecy injunction. In addition there can be the name of the scribe, his father and ancestor, where and when the tablet was written, what it was copied from, where it was deposited, and a sequence of intimidating curses to make sure the tablet is never stolen.

The most famous library tags are those of Ashurbanipal himself, for it is there that we see him boast of his own attainments in cuneiform lore:

> *I learnt the lore of the wise sage Adapa, the hidden secret, the whole of the scribal craft. I can discern celestial and terrestrial portents and deliberate in the assembly of the experts... I can solve convoluted reciprocals and calculations that do not come out evenly. I have read cunningly written text in Sumerian, dark Akkadian, the interpretation of which is difficult. I have examined stone inscriptions from before the Flood, which are sealed, stopped up and mixed up.*

Mental gymnastics

One interesting feature about first millennium BC colophons is a sprightly tendency among the scribes to employ learned or even cryptographic spellings. A recently decrypted example uses the sign UD to stand for no fewer than eight other signs. How to interpret this behaviour is uncertain; it may be to bamboozle rivals or even to show off; probably a mixture of the two. For a modern scholar the pleasure of finally deciphering one of these enduring conundrums is considerable.

In addition, there was a fancy idea in the first millennium that each cuneiform sign had its corresponding number, and whole sentences – especially in omens – could be written in such numbers, so that the reader had to supply the signs for each in his mind (and also select the correct reading for the context). This is already a mental stretch; the matter is confounded by the fact that there were at least *three* different number systems like this in circulation.

Along with the straightforward methods of writing the Akkadian word *šarru*, meaning 'king', appears the use of a large cuneiform number that, intriguingly, can be written in two possible ways:

1. 𒐉𒌋𒌋 = (3 x 60) x (2 x 10) = 180 x 20 = 3,600

2. 𒌋𒌋𒌋𒐉 = (3 x 10) x (2 x 60) = 30 x 120 = 3,600

In Sumerian, the number 3,600 is pronounced 'šar,' and this is used as a pun to write the Akkadian word *šarru*, 'king.'

A weakness for extracting more than one meaning out of a sequence of cuneiform signs probably characterized many professional scribes. The very complication that so troubled the apprentice – that each sign had many possible uses – opened up exciting possibilities to the accomplished scholar. It is this feature that generated the highest-level cuneiform productions, what we call rather uninspiringly 'commentary texts,' in which traditional works that have become obscure or uncertain in meaning are subjected to new and sometimes quite brilliant interpretation. The signs that make up a word can each have their own meaning to contribute, and other devices allowed the deft commentator to bring in references from other compositions, or quote from little-known writings with which he happened to be familiar. Here are a couple of simple examples:

Fig. 29 The non-cuneiform signs stamped at the end of this clay cylinder record the name and titles of King Esarhaddon (680–669 BC) and were only in use for a short period. They were probably developed in the royal chancery in imitation of hieroglyphic inscriptions encountered in Egypt on military campaigns. Clay, 670 BC. Diam. of face: 11 cm. British Museum 78223.

Omen 1:

If a snake encircles the door or bolt in a man's house and won't allow it to open, that house will prosper; secondly it will be abandoned.

Sense explanation: *For a noble it is a good sign; for a commoner it is a bad sign.*

Omen 2:

If the exorcist sees an ox horn on the way to a sick person, that sick person will die.

Sign explanation: The Akkadian word for horn, *qarnu*, is written with the Sumerian logogram SI (see p. 83). The same logogram can mean *nūru*, 'light, *šarūru*, 'brilliance.' So the omen really conveys 'his light will be dimmed.'

Tablets of this kind preserve for us a glimpse of what we might think of as postgraduate teaching two and a half thousand years ago, with the multi-level insights of the *ummânu* or teacher digested and recorded by a student.

Master craftsmen

The royal Assyrian scribes whose handwriting has already been extolled were calligraphers by any criterion, for the layout and details of their documents exemplify mastery of writing on clay and, in addition, a deep sense of the flow and interrelations of the graphic signs as they took their place on the line in sequence. Words could under no circumstances be divided over two lines, and a given text ideally filled front and back of its tablet completely without squashing the signs together or suddenly getting smaller. Texts were conventionally right justified, and an especially un-crowded line could permit the scribe, if he wished, to indulge in an unconventional lengthening of a sign to avoid empty space.

Fig. 30 (Overleaf) A good scribe took great pains when it came to mapping property layouts, so that in future no one could squabble over boundaries. Clay, c.1800 BC. 7.6 x 10.2 cm. British Museum 86394.

Mastery of reed stylus and prepared clay also involved
other skills, although here the evidence is but slight. A
handful of known tablets illustrate what in modern terms
are line drawings: delicate productions drawn with a point,
confident with curves and fluent, to caricature boring
teachers (see fig. 12) or depict demons or ghosts to be
represented as clay figurines. What is interesting here is that
the facility involved implies a level of training and practice
that can only be guessed at, but draughtsmanship was
undoubtedly a substantial element in scribal upbringing.
Maps, too, reflect something of this skill, and here more
examples survive. Indeed, map-making can swerve between
a skeletal outline of a plot of land to be sold, a map of
a whole city, and a map of the whole world, including
all the unknown bits round the edge where no man would
ever go, boldly or otherwise.

The art of writing in reverse must likewise not be
underestimated. Beyond cutting brick stamps, it was also a
special skill needed for preparing personal cylinder seals.
Seals were cut from expensive stone, and were an important
feature of a person's apparel; they could also be handed
down the generations. Seals functioned as a personal
signature when legal procedures needed to be witnessed or
ratified; they would be rolled across the face of a tablet, and
sometimes even right across the writing. Seal cutters with
their design books in the market needed to provide
individualized names, titles and fathers' names for their
customers. The template for these had to be drawn out in
reverse, a confusing proposition for which a proper scribe
on hand must have been essential.

Fig. 31 A great rarity. This scribe has drawn and labelled images of five
sacred cult objects relating to local deities in a temple in the city of
Kish. Despite the tablet's incomplete state, the scribe's ability as a
draughtsman on clay is evident. The kingly figure to the left is possibly
the main god, Zababa, otherwise called Marduk. Clay, c.5th–4th
century BC. 8.9 x 7.2 cm. British Museum 33055.

Fig. 32 When seals were not available, witnesses could make their mark with the curved impressions of the edge of their thumbnail. Many tablets have 'nailmarks' of this kind which were actually made with a tool. Here the witness adds his nail impression 'in place of his cylinder seal' on the left edge of the tablet. Clay, 13th century BC. 4.8 x 7.1 cm. British Museum 17626.

Fig. 33 Seal impression on the top of a tablet: The priest Lipit-Ishtar's seal relies on powerful images for protection; the signs, carefully cut in reverse, give his name, that of his father, Shamash-tappashu, and his profession. Clay, c.19th century BC. 7.4 x 14.7 cm. British Museum 82423.

CHAPTER SIX

What happened to cuneiform?

The idea travels

Fig. 34 A true marvel:
Mesopotamian
cuneiform and
Egyptian hieratic
side-by-side on one
tablet. Tushratta of
Mitanni complains to
Amenhotep III of
Egypt about overdue
dowry payments. The
only possible medium
of communication is
Akkadian. Clay, 14th
century BC. 5 x 9 cm.
British Museum
E29793.

There can be no doubt that, to a contemporary eye, cuneiform looks a touch difficult, although, as previously remarked, it is perhaps easy to exaggerate the level of difficulty that learning it involved in antiquity. Nevertheless it is intriguing that, in the pre-alphabetic world of the second millennium BC where no script other than Egyptian hieroglyphic seems to have attained stable status, cuneiform writing spread far beyond the heartland between the Euphrates and Tigris rivers. Already in the third millennium BC, trained scribes from ancient Iraq made their way outwards to the outlying countries of the Near East, seeking their fortune, exporting cuneiform practice and knowledge. As a result we can observe the scribes who were at work in the Syrian kingdom of Ebla in about 2350 BC who copied imported geographical lists from far away that included the names of small villages in southern Iraq that they could never have heard of or needed or even understood.

This export process increased over time, with the

result that many second millennium rulers in peripheral
states felt the urge to add a cuneiform reader to their staff,
to handle international correspondence and perhaps instil
familiarity with practical writing that would be useful in
many other ways. At the same time, forms of Akkadian
written in cuneiform became the lingua franca of the
entire Near East, exemplified in the royal correspondence
that circulated around the court at Egyptian Amarna in
the fourteenth century BC, transmitting grievances from
the outlying empire whose local kings expected more
attentiveness in their overlords. Elsewhere we can identify
itinerant scribes who could export their professional
knowledge and start a local school with little more than a
bag of reference tablets. The consequence of all this to-ing
and fro-ing was that cuneiform, impressed into clay, never
mind what writing alternatives might have taken root
elsewhere, became the centrally-placed, default writing
system of the whole Near-Eastern world.

A babbling of tongues

The venerable Mesopotamian cuneiform syllabary was
thus adopted and adapted during the second millennium
BC to write languages for which it was never intended,
including Hittite in Anatolia, Urartian in Armenia, Elamite
in Iran and Hurrian in Syria. It is interesting that, despite
its complexity, cuneiform script had sufficient flexibility to
enable application to such completely unrelated languages.
This state of affairs also had other consequences.

Fig. 35 Hittite scribes had to learn Sumerian and Akkadian as foreign languages. They wrote syllabically in cuneiform mixed with words in Sumerian and Akkadian. Some texts also contained Hurrian and Hattic words. Clay c.1200 BC. 24.5 x 20.6 cm. British Museum 108548.

At thirteenth century Ugarit, the development of a
streamlined alphabet was unable to detach itself from the
concept that writing necessarily involved cuneiform wedges
impressed into clay, even though the sign repertoire was
vastly simpler and quite independent of the Mesopotamian
parent. In the same way the Old Persian alphabetic
cuneiform later used at Bisutun by Darius that we have

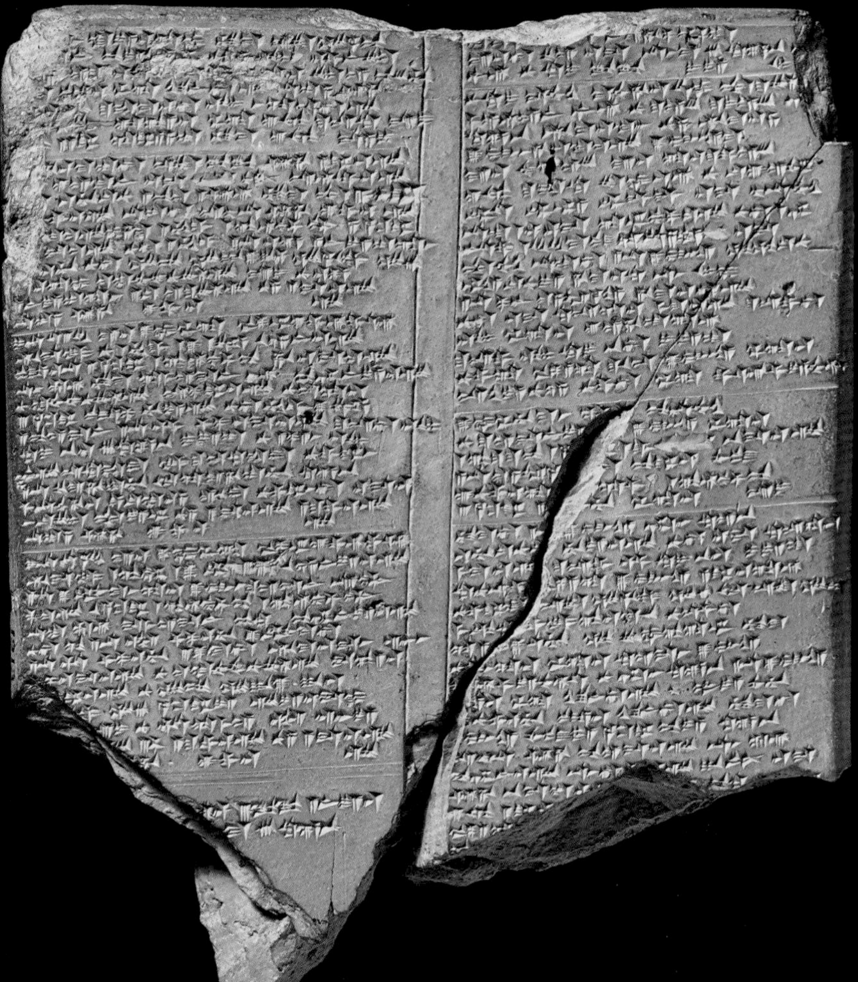

Figs 36–39 Each of these varieties derives from Mesopotamian cuneiform, and has its own defining characteristics. All entail a simplification of the original system. Images are not to scale but dimensions follow. On page 68: (above) Urartian cuneiform. Stone, c.700 BC. 59.8 x 52 cm. British Museum 90863; (below) Old Persian cuneiform. Stone, 5th century BC. 61 x 34.2 cm. British Museum 118840. On page 69: (above) Hurrian gods. Clay, c.1200 BC. 4.9 x 5 cm. British Museum 108620; (below) Elamite cuneiform. Cast. 6th century BC. 30.5 x 17.8 cm. British Museum C44.

already mentioned developed out of wedges written on
clay. Perhaps, too, Mycenaean Linear B, written on clay in
syllabic signs, also drew inspiration from Mesopotamian
cuneiform tradition.

As the first millennium proceeded it is clear that
Aramaic, a sister language to Semitic Babylonian, gradually
came to predominate as the local spoken language of
ancient Iraq. We can document its presence in sporadic
Aramaic loanwords in cuneiform, Aramaic subscripts in ink
on traditional clay documents, and a single school text in
which the Aramaic alphabet, in its modern abecedary
(alphabetic) order, was expressed by cuneiform syllables
as an innovative scribal exercise. The whole process was
accelerated by the military takeover of Babylon by Cyrus
the Great of Persia (559–530 BC) in 539 BC, for the Persians
imposed Aramaic as the functional language of state
administration throughout their rapidly developing empire.

Despite these new linguistic and literary forces
cuneiform defiantly held its own in the face of the new
possibilities raised by an alphabet, its resistance bolstered
by the huge traditional lore preserved in the libraries of
clay, coupled with an understandable reluctance to change.
On another level it must be stressed that our modern view
that writing should be within the reach of everyone never
prevailed in the ancient Near-Eastern world; no one ever
proclaimed that this should be the case, and it is likely that,
if anything, the 'establishment' would have seen no social
advantage in the idea. Knowledge, after all, is power, and
there was a great deal of venerable knowledge available in
cuneiform texts.

The last wedge

We can follow writing on clay all the way down to the
first century AD, in the form of astronomical texts. It is
certainly significant that the academies in which the pursuit

of astrology and astronomy endured should prove to be the
last bastion of the old system of writing. It was resources of
this kind that brought Greek scholars to Babylon, lured by
the reputation of the 'Chaldean' scholars as observers of the
heavens; some presumably, even learned a little cuneiform,
using tablets such as the one in fig. 41. Here the men of
Athens met calculations vested exclusively in the timeless
Mesopotamian system of sexagesimal counting; their liberal
borrowing imposed the measuring in sixties that has prevailed
ever since when it comes to seconds, minutes and the degrees
of a circle. Interchange with the Greeks came just in time;
the day came when the last old cuneiformist breathed his
last, and the noble gift of some three and a half thousand
years of wedge-writing for mankind came to an end.

CHAPTER SEVEN

How did it work?

Cuneiform was real writing. It could express anything the scribes wanted to say. Over its history each character could take any one of dozens of shapes, and could have many different uses. But in reality, the variety that existed in any situation was limited. What makes cuneiform difficult to read today is the extinction of the languages written in it, the irretrievable loss of the contexts behind the documents, and the alien nature of the technology, customs and beliefs of the ancient authors. Worst of all, many of our sources are worn or broken.

Mind over material

Cuneiform signs are made up of combinations of wedges produced by impressing a reed stylus into the surface of a fresh tablet of clay. Reeds and clay had always been freely available in the rivers alongside which Mesopotamian cities grew. Scribes read by holding the tablet in such a way that sunlight cast shadows into the wedges.

Stylus

The stylus (*qanû* 'reed') was literally cut from a length of
reed, as is regularly revealed by the impressions left in the
clay in tablets across Mesopotamian history (see fig. 43).
There are grooves in the left edge of each wedge, while
the right is smooth; the top edge has several small, circular
marks. The markings are made by the fibrous structure of
the reed, the smooth edge is its outer skin.

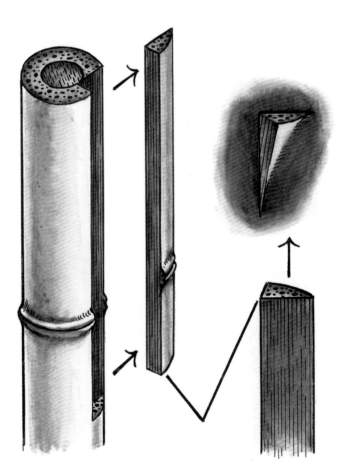

Fig. 42 How a stylus
was cut from a reed;
and the tell-tale marks
left behind inside
each wedge.

Fig. 43 The grooves and circular marks made by the reed stylus are visible in these wedges. See fig. 42. The left-most wedge is 4 mm high. *c.*1800 BC. British Museum 16953.

Clay and tablet

Tablet clay is not as fine as that used by modern potters; it is essentially river mud, brought down by the spring floods of the Tigris and Euphrates rivers. Scribes always knew where to find the right quality of clay for their needs. Ephemeral documents could be written on rougher clay, while library tablets could be written on finer clay, sometimes so smoothly finished as to look like porcelain. Most tablets were left to dry in the air, although not in the full sun. In special cases, some were baked to ensure their survival. It is evident that this process was fully understood.

Tablets were very carefully made; it was a skill that needed practice. Fig. 44 shows a tablet made by rolling out thin sheets of clay. First a sheet was folded over itself into a small rectangle shape. The fold is visible from left to right across the bottom of the photo, and the end flap at the left end. Then this rectangle was placed on another sheet of clay, at ninety degrees. This second sheet was folded over the first. These folds are visible along the centre of the photo.

Fig. 44 Below is a list of chairs being accounted for by a large institution in the southern Mesopotamian city of Girsu around 2000 BC. Small documents like this survive in staggering numbers. The short-lived empire known as the Third Dynasty of Ur (or Ur III; so-called because of an ancient list of kings and their home cities) is notorious for the detail in which its administrators recorded their activities. Around 100,000 tablets, maybe one in five of all known tablets, date to this period, most to within not much more than a single generation. Examples can be found today in countless museum collections across the world. Clay. 38 x 51 cm. British Museum 26783.

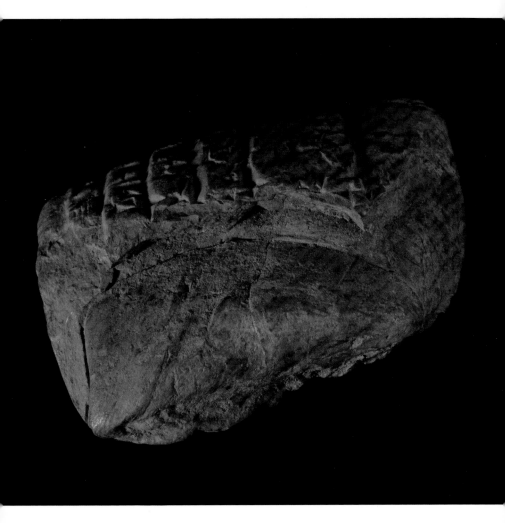

Fig. 45 (Above) Stylus impressed into clay, making the wedge-shaped impressions that give cuneiform its modern name.

Fig. 46 (Below) Occasionally, the clay displaced in making one wedge distorts the depression already made by another. This photo and the diagram below reveal how scribes were trained to write the wedges in each sign in a particular order, as is the case with pen strokes in Chinese writing. Detail from K.1662 showing three signs.

There were conventions for sizes and shapes of tablet, depending on the kind of text, and when and where it was being written. There were also different conventions for how to set the text out on the tablet surface. The combination of these features is usually enough to allow a specialist to identify roughly what a text is, and when and where it was written, before even reading a single sign of cuneiform. Tablets were designed for human use. Most fit comfortably into the palm of a hand, and are not very heavy. Ergonomically, they are like mobile phones.

Writing

When it came to the moment of inscription, the important thing was to judge the point at which the clay would best take a sharp impression, without being too hard or too soft. For very long texts, the clay would need to have been kept moist. There are three basic types of wedge made, depending on the orientation at which the stylus is held to the tablet:

1) vertical ⊤   2) horizontal ▶—   3) oblique ◀

Having mastered those, it is possible to write any of the signs in the repertoire. To make a wedge, the scribe pushed the corner of the stylus end into the surface of the clay at a low angle; the greater the pressure, the deeper and bigger the wedge. When a longer wedge was desired, the shaft of the stylus could be pivoted down to make greater contact with the surface. The length of the wedge is determined by how much of the shaft meets the clay.

What is made is the characteristic wedge-shaped ('cuneiform') impression. The stylus was then lifted out of the clay again ready to make the next wedge. The whole writing process is one of pressing. There was no dragging the stylus across the clay, as we do with a pen on paper.

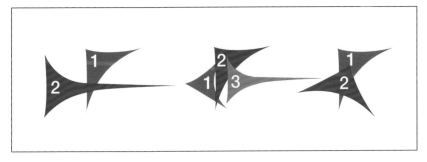

Figs 47 and 48 (Opposite and overleaf) King Ashurnasirpal of Assyria (883–859 BC) had texts glorifying his achievements carved into the walls of his luxurious new palace in Nimrud. One text was written so many times that it has earned the modern nickname of 'the Standard Inscription'; most examples of it were left behind by the early excavators. Stone, c.875–860 BC. 127 x 224 cm. British Museum 124561.

Tablets were inscribed carefully. Roughly made or written tablets were suitable for scribbled notes, but not for official or professional documentation, or even personal letters. Scribes made mistakes just as we do today. Some went unnoticed. They can reveal the pronunciation of a word or show how the scribe went about writing his tablet. Other mistakes were left uncorrected. Erasing mistakes on clay was actually quite difficult because the wedges were impressed so deeply. Removing them meant disturbing so much clay that the scribe risked erasing a lot of other text, too. Erasures are obvious from the disturbance of the clay and from the deep traces of wedges that remain under the newly inscribed sign. The best policy was to avoid the mistake in the first place.

In the king's name

Cuneiform was not an alphabet, but a system that wrote syllables and words. Cuneiform signs characteristically cannot express isolated consonants without an attached vowel. It used between 600 and 1000 different characters (called 'signs' in the scholarly jargon), although about 100 or so were quite enough for most purposes. While cuneiform was wonderfully suited to writing on clay, it was also sometimes carved into stone or engraved into metal. These materials were scarce in Mesopotamia, which made them expensive and prestigious. Cuneiform written on hard materials mimicked its appearance on clay, although the handwriting was deliberately old fashioned. Here we see Ashurnasirpal's name, which is written with five signs:

m   aš-   šur-   PAP.   A

In Akkadian his name (outlined above) is *Aššur nāṣir apli*, which means '[the god] Ashur is protector of the heir', the heir in question being Ashurnasirpal himself. The first sign, ^m𒁹, is the number 1. Here it is used as a determinative, a special type of silent character, telling the reader that what comes next is the name of a person (rendered here '^m' for masculine). That god's name is Ashur, the chief god of Assyria, written syllabically with two signs, AŠ 𒀸 and ŠUR 𒋩. Next comes PAP 𒉽, which represents a whole word using a Sumerian logogram. The reader needs both to supply the corresponding Akkadian word and work out from the context the appropriate form (like when we encounter '$' in an English text). Here the word is *naṣāru* 'to protect', and the required form *nāṣir* 'protector'.

We have just explored the first principle of cuneiform – a cuneiform sign can potentially be used: 1) to clarify

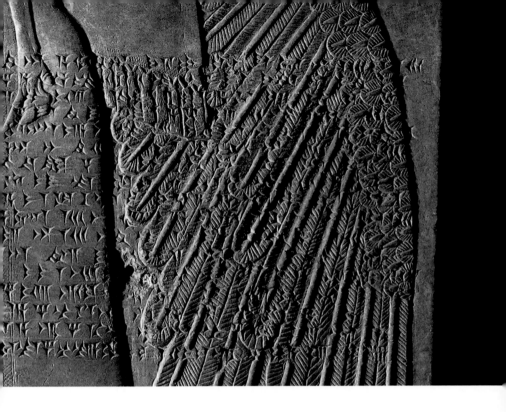

what kind of thing a word represents (determinative);
2) to convey a sound (syllable); 3) to write a whole word
(logogram).

Now let's look at the second principle: cuneiform signs
can have more than one 'reading'; that is, each may
represent any of a choice of sounds or words. The last
character in Ashurnasirpal's name, A𒀀, can be used either
as a simple syllable, /a/ or as a whole word. A in Sumerian
means 'water'. In an Akkadian text we would read A as
their word for water, *mû*. When writing names, however,
the same sign can be used to express instead the Akkadian
word *aplu* 'heir'.

Finally, the third principle of cuneiform: one sound
can be written with different signs. For example, the sound
/du/ can be written with the following signs, among others,
which we today differentiate with index numbers:

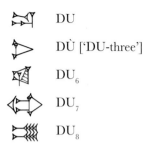

The sign DU was used for the Sumerian verb 'to go' (or its Akkadian equivalent, *alāku*); DÙ is 'to build'; DU₆ 'ruin mound'; DU₇ 'to be suitable'; DU₈ 'to open'. In Sumerian there are many such groups of homophonous words (that is, words sounding similar to each other). While sometimes one sign can be found as a variant for another, spelling habits generally kept each member of these groups of signs distinct from the others. This is advantageous. Ironically, syllabically written Sumerian is far harder for us to understand than text written in a mix of words and syllables. We don't always know how logographically written words would have been pronounced. It is sometimes thought that Sumerian may have been a tonal language (like Chinese), making homophonous words more distinct for them than they appear to us, and to ancient speakers of – non-tonal – Akkadian. Our knowledge of Sumerian is still often influenced by reading it with the help of Akkadian resources such as ancient sign lists (see chapter 4; fig. 24), which use DU to show the pronounciation of all the other DU-signs.

These defining features of cuneiform – where one sign can be read in different ways and different signs can have the same reading – are often cited as reasons why cuneiform is impossibly difficult to learn. In reality, it is rarely that troublesome. We overcome similar problems without a second thought. For example, in English writing TH expresses both the sound in **THE** and that in **THIEF**, as well as two sounds in SHOR**THA**ND. The second situation is like English using PH, GH and F for the sound /f/ (as in **PH**ISHING, ENOU**GH** and **F**ISH). And context usually makes the right reading clear in less familiar instances.

Hardback volumes

Clay tablets survive remarkably well in Iraq. As unfired clay, they could be recycled by soaking in water. In practice, many were just thrown away. Most of the hundreds of thousands of tablets we have were never intended to last for more than a few years. They were found as ancient rubbish of one form or another. By contrast, organic materials such as wood and ivory rarely survive at all. Yet we know that scribes did sometimes use them instead of clay tablets. From around 2100 BC scribes used some kind of writing boards.

The best surviving specimens of writing boards, still containing a few inscribed patches, were found at the eighth century BC Assyrian city of Nimrud. They owe their survival to the fact that they were thrown down a well when the city was destroyed in 612 BC. The boards are made of small sheets of wood with the middle carved out so that a rim remained around the edges. Wax would be poured into the depression. If need be, several such sheets could be bound together into a kind of hardback book. The scribe would write on the wax in the same way as on clay. Writing boards would have been a convenient tool to carry around when out of the office, a bit like writing on a clipboard. The Assyrian scribes shown in the palace reliefs often carry boards instead of tablets.

Other boards from Nimrud were much larger, around 30 x 15 cm, and must have been sumptuous. Scientific testing revealed that they were made of walnut. Such boards were used not just as scratchpads, but also for copying scholarly texts. Library records (on clay tablets)

Fig. 49 Luxury ivory writing boards from Nimrud. These leaves were from a set of sixteen once bound together. They held an astrological textbook called *Enuma Anu Enlil*. This set belonged to King Sargon II of Assyria (721–705 BC), and must originally have been part of his palace collection in Khorsabad. Ivory, *c*.720–710 BC. 16 x 34 cm. British Museum 131952 and 131953.

Figs 50–51 Two small fragments from Ashurbanipal's Library show us that ink must have been used much more widely than we had expected. Here the librarian has written a statement of library ownership on tablets received from other collections. Clay, 7th century BC. 6.7 x 6.7 cm and 2.2 x 3.2 cm. British Museum DT 273 and K 10100.

from seventh-century Nineveh tell us that many of the
books being brought into King Ashurbanipal's famous
library were written on boards, perhaps because the
donors did not want to part with their original tablets.

Now you see it, now you don't

Throughout history there have been close ties between
a spoken language, the script in which that language is
written, and the technology used to write it. In the case
of the Sumerian and Akkadian languages, cuneiform
was the script used, and clay and stylus the standard
technology. Cuneiform scribes operated in a
world that knew the use of ink; they had used
it themselves for various purposes for many
centuries. But only rarely did they write
cuneiform in ink, as far as we know. Ink is
another material that survives poorly in
Mesopotamia. Scribes did write cuneiform
in ink as part of palace decoration, for
example. More intriguingly, two tablets
from Nineveh show inked cuneiform
on clay tablets (figs 50–51). The ink was
used to write colophons (see chapter 3),
presumably because the tablet in each case
had become too dry. The proficiency shown there
suggests that they were already familiar with writing
in ink. From the final days of cuneiform, the last few
centuries BC and the first century AD, there is also evidence
to suggest wider use of ink. Clay tablets preserve
mention of parchments containing traditional
Mesopotamian texts which must have been
written in ink. It is highly likely that these texts
were written in the traditional languages, and
in cuneiform. But the documents themselves
do not survive.

CHAPTER EIGHT

Counting days

Once upon a time

The Mesopotamian year (usually) started in spring, about March–April, as it traditionally has in many parts of the world. The month started after the first sighting of the new moon, and would last for 29 or 30 days. The day started at sunset, and moved through 'watches' until the next sunset. We know less about how time itself was measured during the day (and night!), but as early as the second millennium Mesopotamians were using sundials and water-clocks. The need to master time is evident in the earliest texts. A sign was created to indicate 'day'. Its shape was based on the image of a sun rising in the east. By adding numbers alongside this sign, scribes could count multiple days. Placing numbers inside the DAY sign indicated instead MONTH. The power of the system increased further: placing numbers through the DAY sign indicated YEAR. The remarkable sophistication of this bureaucracy is highlighted by tablets covering multiple years. The sign for DAY was used until the very end of cuneiform.

Fig. 52 In each line down the left side of this tablet is the sign for DAY plus a number, from 1 up to 5. Each line thus represents a day's transactions. Clay, c.3000 BC. 7.8 x 7.8 cm. British Museum 116730.

As a picture of the sun, it remained in use as a sign for the sun(-god), too. MONTH also remained. It took the form of DAY with the number 30 written inside, representing a thirty-day lunar month. MONTH was not used to write the moon-god's name, but the number 30 sometimes was.

Calendars

The Mesopotamian year had twelve months in a year. Month names referred to typical activities for that season, such as *še-kin-kud* 'harvesting the grain'. There was a slight problem, though. The time it takes for the earth to revolve around the sun – a solar year – is around 11 days longer than a lunar year (12 lunar months). Our Gregorian calendar suffers a similar problem; we add an extra day to February every four years (except for every 100 years, but including every 400 years). In Babylonia, the solution was similar. Every so often, an extra month was added. These were known as *diri* ('extra') months. Originally they were introduced as and when the need was felt, but later (based on astronomical observations) a regular pattern was devised. Different cities used different calendars. Some month names were shared between cities, although not necessarily used in the same order; other names were unique to a city.

Counting years was a little more complicated: nobody knew they were BC. There was no epoch-making moment from which each year was counted. One system gave names to each year. The king and his counsellors would discuss the significant events of the past year and choose one to be commemorated in the name of the next. For example, Amar-Suen's fourth year (*c.*2043 BC) was known as: 'Year [celebrating]: *Enmahgalanna* has been chosen as *en*-priestess of the god Nanna by means of the omens'. When no event surpassed the significance of the one

immortalized last time around, the next year would be
'the year after' the previous one. Rim-Sin of Larsa was
so proud of his decisive victory over the rival kingdom
of Isin (*c.*1792 BC) that he named his next thirty years
after it.

When years have commemorative names instead of
numbers, how does anyone know what to call the next
year? Simple: scribes were sent tablets telling them the
next name. And to help them remember the order of
years – necessary for loans, house purchases and any
other medium- to long-term commitments – they kept
lists of which year followed which (see fig. 53). These are
very helpful for modern scholars. Each kingdom chose
their own names, meaning that any given year could be
called several different things from one city to the next.

Starting around 1595 BC, with the arrival of the
Kassite dynasty in Babylonia, scribes would simply count
from the accession of each new ruler. The Assyrians
preferred a system where high officials drew lots to decide
who would give his own name to the new year. For
example, Bel-bunaya, the palace herald, gave his name
to 850 BC. In the last years of cuneiform, a more familiar
system appeared: the Seleucid Era counted each year
from a start date of 311 BC. The alignment of ancient
years to modern ones is based partly on astronomy.
A solar eclipse recorded in 763 BC gives us secure dates
from then on, and historical records get us back to
around 1400 BC, with little room for disagreement.
Before that, we have floating sections of time where we
(often) know the order of years, but we don't know for
sure exactly when they actually happened. Some of
them may have overlapped. History is still being written.

Counting in 60s

Cuneiform was invented as a bookkeeping tool (not for literature, glorification of kings or gods, diaries or shopping lists). The original sign for 'scribe' appears to be a picture of an abacus-like counting board on which clay tokens representing commodities would have been moved around. The early number signs seem to be based on such tokens, which were in use already during the prehistoric period. There were many different counting systems, depending on what was being counted: lengths, areas, capacities and quantities of discrete commodities. These continued in use, although the exact size of a capacity might change from time to time. Some of these systems were based on the number 60, and even those that weren't gradually took on elements of the 60-system.

Around 2100 BC a new counting system was invented that had profound implications both for Mesopotamians and for us today. It was fully abstract and meant that anything could be calculated – in 60s – quickly and easily using just this one system. The scribes who used it worked with an administrative fiction of each year having 360 days. It is ultimately this system that explains why we have 60 minutes in an hour and 360 degrees in a circle. These scribes, however, used it only for calculations,

Fig. 53 Scribes constantly updated reference lists of year names, to help them keep track of the passage of time. This list records and totals twenty year names, from the thirtieth year of Hammurapi to the sixth of his successor, Samsu-iluna. The full form of year names was often very long. When dating documents, scribes tended to use shorter forms such as those found here. Samsu-iluna's first year (c.1750 BC), 'Year: Samsu-iluna the king, by the true command of the god Marduk has made his lordship manifest in all the lands, and has made prosper the people of Sumer and Akkad', would become simply 'Year: the true command'. Clay, c.1744 BC. 5.1×9.2 cm. British Museum 96695.

converting figures from the traditional systems, doing some maths, and then converting the answer back into the appropriate traditional signs.

Individual records were summarized into annual registers. In fig. 55, the scribe gives the name and size of individual fields within one district of the city of Umma, the name of the person managing each, and the yields, for the third year of Ibbi-Sin's reign (*c*.2026 BC). Over 2,000 hectares are accounted for here, producing two million litres of cereals. Tablets like this one are among the largest known, weighing in at around 8kg each. At this period managers were set (tough!) targets each year based on assumptions of productivity per man per day. Any shortfall or surplus was carried forward into the following year, in a meticulous balanced accounting system.

Scribes needed to manipulate small numbers as well as large. At school they practised fractions. Cuneiform maths was based on two symbols: ⟍(1) and ⟨ (10). ⟍ was not just 1, but also 60 or any power of 60, in the same way that for us 1 indicates one unit (i.e. 1), one ten (**10**) or one hundred (**100**) and so on, as well as 0.**1**, 0.0**1** etc. Cuneiform had no zero and no 'point'; numbers in this system were relative. ⟨⟍ is most simply 11 (10+1), but could equally be taken as 39600 (10 x (60 x 60) + 1 x (60 x 60)) or 0.183 (10 x (1 ÷ 60)) … ⟍⟨ is most simply 70 (60+10). This list of fractions tells you to start with 60 (we know it is 60 not 1

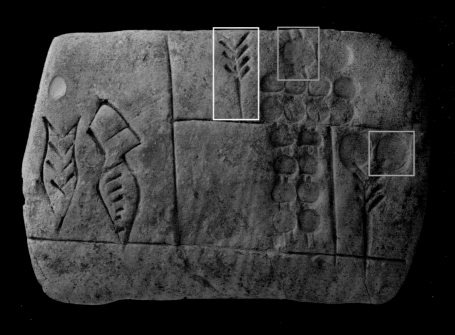

because some copies write a sound clue, as we might write '60^{ty}'; cuneiform fractions are thus $60/n$ not $1/n$), then divide that by the numbers in the left hand column ('it's n-th part'), writing the answers in the right-hand column. The idea is to work out pairs of numbers that multiplied together give the answer 60. Line two on the tablet, for example, says 𝕿𝕿𝕿 (3) ◁◁ (20). This effectively reads $60 \div 3 = 20$. Fractions have intimidated schoolchildren since they were first invented. The advantage of the Mesopotamian system is that there are plenty of numbers that you can divide 60 by and end up with a whole number answer ($60/30 = 2$; $60/20 = 3$; $60/15 = 4$; $60/12 = 5$; $60/10 = 6 \ldots$).

110116
1914
4-4
182

Fig. 55 Annual register as discussed on p. 94. Clay, c.2026 BC. 31.1 x 31.8 cm. British Museum 110116.

Fig. 56 A well-preserved list of 'fractions' from the hand of a good student. Clay, *c.*2000 BC. 4.5 x 8.5 cm. British Museum 106444.

Fig. 57 The *Sumerian King List*, a piece of state propaganda, attributes to the earliest rulers of Sumer reigns tens of thousands of years long. Clay, *c.*1800 BC. 7.4 x 13 cm. British Museum 108857.

CHAPTER NINE

Why study cuneiform?

In our very modern world, far in time from that of the ancient Sumerians and Babylonians, it might seem a fair question to ask why we should bother with their old and strange-looking writings and struggle to translate them. Can anything really come out of them of use or interest to us today?

Cuneiform is the world's oldest writing system. Writing it on clay meant that even the most ephemeral of messages over more than five thousand years old could survive safely in the ground awaiting the archaeologist's spade. Museums and collections round the world look after such documents in abundance, overseeing their condition, storing them safely, indexing and cataloguing them. Thanks to the valiant efforts of the early decipherers and all the scholars who came after, we can understand these writings today with remarkable accuracy. We can listen in on the most

ancient voices, from kings to schoolboys, from direct
records of their daily lives and experiences. We hear of
their wars and history, but also their thoughts and
ambitions, their enquiries about the world that surrounded
them, and their understanding of how it worked. We can
walk beside their mathematicians and astronomers as well
as their doctors and astrologers. Cuneiform tablets of clay
may be unfamiliar at first sight – and they are sometimes
hard-to-read – but what they preserve for us is, quite simply,
wonderful. Ancient humanity, as we encounter it face
to face in documents from Mesopotamia, can be
disconcertingly familiar, and there are still lessons to
be learned.

Try this at home!

Writing cuneiform is surprisingly easy. All you need is
your tablet, made of modelling clay or plasticine, and
your stylus, for which you can use almost any squared
off tool, perhaps a chopstick, ice-cream stick or the reed
from a clarinet.

Choose your words and divide them up into syllables,
such as *ta-ab-le-et* (see chart overleaf). Remember: you
cannot write a consonant (such as *h*, *m* or *s*) on its own,
but there are cuneiform signs when you need a single
vowel, such as in ***a**-da-am*. Not all of the sounds you need
are available in cuneiform (there is no *c* or *j*, for example),
so you will need to find a close approximate sound. The
ancients faced the same problem when they encountered
people who spoke other languages which also used sounds
that were not catered for in cuneiform.

AB	BA	EB	BE
AD	DA	ED	DE
AG	GA	EG	GE
AH	HA	EH	HE
AK	KA	EK	KE
AL	LA	EL	LE
AM	MA	EM	ME
AN	NA	EN	NE
AP	PA	EP	PE
AQ	QA	EQ	QE
AR	RA	ER	RE
AS	SA	ES	SE
AT	TA	ET	TE
AZ	ZA	EZ	ZE

IB	BI	UB	BU	A
ID	DI	UD	DU	E
IG	GI	UG	GU	I
IH	HI	UH	HU	U
IK	KI	UK	KU	
IL	LI	UL	LU	
IM	MI	UM	MU	
IN	NI	UN	NU	
IP	PI	UP	PU	
IQ	QI	UQ	QU	
IR	RI	UR	RU	
IS	SI	US	SU	
IT	TI	UT	TU	
IZ	ZI	UZ	ZU	

Where to find out more

Cuneiform

Charpin, D., *Reading and Writing in Babylon*
(Harvard University Press, 2010)
Radner, K. and E. Robson (eds), *The Oxford Handbook of Cuneiform Culture* (Oxford University Press, 2011)

Culture

Crawford, H. (ed.), *The Sumerian World* (Routledge, 2013)
Curtis, J. and J. Reade (eds), *Art and Empire: Treasures from Assyria in the British Museum* (British Museum Press, 1995)
Finkel, I. and M. Seymour (eds), *Babylon, Myth and Reality* (British Museum Press, 2008)
Leick, G. (ed.), *The Babylonian World* (Routledge, 2007)
Sasson, J.M. (ed.), *Civilizations of the Ancient Near East* (Scribner, 1995)

History

Roux, G., *Ancient Iraq* (George Allen & Unwin, 1964)
Van de Mieroop, M., *A History of the Ancient Near East, ca.3000–323 BC* (Blackwell Publishing, 2004)

Literature

Black, J. A., G. Cunningham, E. Robson and
G. Zolyomi (eds), *The Literature of Ancient Sumer*
(Oxford University Press, 2004)
Foster, B.R., *Before the Muses: An Anthology of
Akkadian Literature* (CDL Press, 1993)

Digital resources

BBCi Ancient History of Mesopotamia:
http://www.bbc.co.uk/history/ancient/cultures/
    mesopotamia_gallery.shtml
Mesopotamia: British Museum educational website
designed to support the Key Stage 2 curriculum:
    http://www.mesopotamia.co.uk/menu.html
Oracc: http://oracc.org
Electronic Text Corpus of Sumerian Literature:
    http://etcsl.orinst.ox.ac.uk/
Etana: http://www.etana.org/home
International Association for Assyriology:
    http://iaassyriology.org/

Index

Picture credits

The majority of objects illustrated in this book are from the collection of the British Museum. Unless otherwise stated below, all photographs are copyright the Trustees of the British Museum and are courtesy of the Museum's Photographic and Imaging Department.